Read Chinese Today

Understanding Chinese Characters by means of their Ancestral Forms

PING-GAM GO

SIMPLEX PUBLICATIONS

SAN FRANCISCO

Acknowledgment

I would like to acknowledge my three daughters Sian, Lan and Hian for their keen interest in this project and for their valuable contributions in submitting material for the manuscript and in making suggestions, corrections and improvements.

My special thanks goes to Ms. Doris Tseng, librarian at the Chinatown branch of the San Francisco Public Library for doing research work on the official translation of the sign at the Chinatown Gate, appearing on page W3.

The brush-written characters (not the ancestral forms, which were done by myself) were done by Mr. You-shan Tang, Peking artist now living here.

My thanks also goes to Ms. Janet Gardiner for accurate proofreading.

Read Chinese Today. Copyright © 1991 by Gam P. Go. All rights reserved. Printed in the Unites States of America. No part of this publication may be used, reproduced in any form or by any electronic or mechanical means (including photocopying, recording, or information storage and retrieval) without permission in writing from the publisher.

ISBN 0-9623113-3-2

Simplex Publications, 11 Hugo Street, San Francisco, CA 94122

PUBLISHER'S NOTE

An expanded version of *Read Chinese Today* by the same author is available under the title *Understanding Chinese Characters, by means of their Ancestral Forms.*

It contains numerous photographs and an expanded Dictionary containig 288 Characters with their Ancestral Forms. A Second Edition is in preparation.

A Walk through San Francisco's Chinatown

This section is a preparation for the *Walk through San Francisco's Chinatown* by explaining the signs to be seen on the basis of their ancestral forms.

The signs contain common Chinese characters that are also commonly seen in other American Chinatowns and cities. *It is therefore not necessary that you do the actual walk yourself, in order to get the benefits from this section.*

I. A Walk through San Francisco's Chinatown.

A short walk through San Francisco's Chinatown will allow us to study and understand 60 common characters. They are very common characters that are used over and over again by the Chinese.

The Entrance Gate to Chinatown bears a sign with a well-known saying by Confucius*: 公 為 下 天 , which written in their ancestral forms would be: 㕣 㲽 丅 天 . Old Chinese writings are read from right to left**. So the first character is 天 , which means **HEAVEN** [i.e. *that which expands* 一 *over* **Man** 大 (*a Man with widespread arms and legs)*]. The second character is 丅 , which means **BELOW** (*an object* | *below a certain level* 一). The third character was originally written 㲽 . It is a picture of a **Female Monkey** with its *claws* 爪 , *body* 冂 and *breasts* ⺀ . The original meaning of this character is lost, but one of its present meanings is **FOR** (**For the benefit of**). Lastly, the last character 公 means **COMMON**, or **PUBLIC**. It represents the *division/distribution* 八 *of private property* (厶 *cocoon*, with the self-enclosed silkworm it gives the idea of privacy) *among the common people*. Putting the four meanings together, we would have " Below Heaven For Common". Freely translated it would be: " Under Heaven We All Must Work for the Common Good" **(Photo A)**

---

* This saying was quoted by **Dr. Sun Yat-Sen** [who led the Revolution that overthrew the Manchu Dynasty (1644-1912)] in one of a series of lectures that he held one year before his death in 1925.

** Writing was done on a roll of paper or silk, with the right hand doing the writing and the left hand holding the roll and unrolling the material. Therefore, writing was done from right to left.

Let us now see characters that we see a lot of times. For instance, we will quite often see these two characters next to each other: 酒家. Originally they were written: 酒家. The first means **Wine** : a *wine jar* and *wine* (*liquid*); the other one means **House(hold)**: a *dwelling* where *pigs* 豕 had free entry ***. The two characters combined mean <u>Wine House</u> or <u>RESTAURANT</u> , namely *one that serves liquor.* (**Photos C, H, J**)

The Chinese have other notations for Restaurants. They often use 宫 if it is big and stylish. It means <u>**Palace**</u> because the original writing is , i.e. a *dwelling* containing a series of (a lot of) rooms . Smaller places quite often call themselves <u>Garden</u> 園 , which was originally written : an *enclosure* , and the symbol inside it, which means *a long robe* * , because the long vines in the garden give the impression as if the trees put on long robes. (**Photo J**) (**Photos C, K**)

<u>A bigger restaurant with *dining rooms upstairs,*</u> will use 樓 : a <u>**Multi-Story Building**</u> . The ancestral form of this character 樓 : a building (*tree* , *wood*) and (a *woman* 女 *locked* up in a *lofty palace prison* for misbehavior)(**Photos F, G**)

Another notation is 飯店; originally written the pair means <u>**Rice Shop**</u> , because the first is the symbol for **Food** or **Cooked Rice** : a *pot with contents* , a *ladle* and the symbol - three lines coming together -

---

* The symbol represents the *shoulder* on which the robe rests; the robe is so long that it is *dragging* (a *hook* attached to the harness, used for dragging objects) over the floor.

** This symbol 卜 represents *cracks* in a tortoise-shell which resulted when it was heated. Divination (fortune-telling) was then spoken out (mouth) after closely studying the cracks.

*** To make sure that they were adequately fed.

to suggest *mixing* ; and ⼺ is a *hand* in *motion* ⼐ which brings the food into one's mouth. The second character ⼐ stands for **Shop** (⼐ *shelter* in which *divination* ** ⼘ is practiced). (**Photo R**, in Flower *Shop*.)

Another combination we'll see is 餐 廳 , of which the ancestral forms are ⼂ ⼂. The first character consists of many symbols, namely ⼂ *food* (a *pot with conents* ⼂ , a *ladle* ⼂ , and ⼂ : three lines coming together to suggest *mixing*); ⼂ a *skeleton* after the flesh is removed (by a *hand* ⼂). All of them put together they mean **Meal**. How about the other one ? A very complex one , it means **Hall**. It is composed of the symbol ⼐ *shelter* and a very complicated portion ⼂ , which means *to hear* and only serves as a "phonetic" (to give the pronunciation of the character). It is used here, because musical performance often takes place here. The two characters combined mean **Meal Hall** , or **Restaurant**. They are often used, because they look very beautiful and distinguished and give a certain dignity to the place. (**Photo S**)

Now that we have learned to understand these characters for "Restaurant", can we remember all of them ? The answer should be "Certainly!", especially if we live in San Francisco, because as can be expected, all these characters appear *at the end of the signs* and we can see and recognize them each time we visit Chinatown !

Here are other "pairs" that we can spot easily. Anywhere we go, we will find these two together: 公 司 , because they mean **FIRM** or **COMPANY**. In their ancestral forms they would look like this: ⼂ ⼂. The first means **Common**: a *division and distribution* ⼂ of private property ⼂ (picture of a *cocoon* ; with the self-enclosed silkworm, it gives the idea of 'privacy'). The second symbol ⼂ is a *man bending over* ⼂ (⼂*man*) *in order to shout his orders* (⼂ mouth), and means **To manage**

---

or **Administration**. Combining the two together, we have **Common Administration**. And is this not the idea behind a Firm or Company ? (**Photo I**)

Another pair that we'll see is that which indicates a **BANK.** This pair 銀行 we'll see often enough.It means **Silver Store**, because probably silver was the metal used as currency. (Gold being only used for decorative purposes and in jewelry.) **Silver** was originally written 銀 . It consists of two parts. The first part is 金 metal**: 金 four pieces of ore buried (∧ cover) in the ground . The other part is 艮 : a man 人 * turning around 尸 , in order to look another man 'defiantly' in the eye θ . The two parts combined mean **Silver**, because silver is malleable and 'defies' the action of a hammer. **Store** was originally written 行 , to mean footsteps ⼻彳 made by left (and right) feet, and represents "a place where people come and go". (**Photos B, D, L, T**)

Walking through Chinatown, we will occasionally see these three characters next to each other displayed in the window of a restaurant 粥 麵 飯 (**Photo U**). Written in their ancestral forms they would look like this: 粥 麵 飯 . The first one means **PORRIDGE**:Rice 米 (four grains of rice that are scattered 火 due to thrashing ⼗) that are thoroughly boiled (steam 弓弓 coming from boiling water). The second character means **NOODLES**. It consists of two portions, of which the second (面 face) only serves as a "phonetic", to give the pronunciation of the character. The first portion 麥 means Wheat : a plant 屮 (picture of a plant with its trunk | branches ∨ and roots ⌒) with ears of grain ⼈⼈; and 夂 which is a man 人 * who advances 刀 * in spite of obstacles ∧

---

* The being that has two legs 人 - only the legs are portrayed. A man who 'advances' : a man 人 deformed 刀 , because of his movement.

** If standing by itself, this symbol means **Gold**.

suggesting the relentless development of the grain. The third character, as we already discussed under "Restaurant", means **COOKED RICE**.[**]Having displayed "Porridge, Noodles and Rice (plates)", the place wants to tell the public that it serves all the dishes the public desires, including porridge, which is rarely served in other restaurants.

Another pair of characters that we'll see is that which shows that a restaurant serves **DIM SUM** 點 心 the Cantonese pastry lunch that is very popular in San Francisco, also among tourists **(Photo E)** . The original writing would be: 點 心 . The second character is a picture of the **Heart** : it shows the *sac* (opened), the *lobes* and *aorta* . The first character means **Speck** or **Dot**. It consists of two parts: the first part 黑 means black (*soot* x deposited by a *smoky fire* 炎 around a *vent* ⊕); the second part serves only as a "phonetic", giving an indication how to pronounce the character. The two characters combined mean literally " speck heart ", which freely translated would be "a little heartiness" or simply "a snack" as we say it.

Several times during the walk, we will encounter the character 華 , which stands for **CHINA** **(Photos C, O, P)**
Originally written 華 , it actually means **Glorious**, being a picture of *a branch with leaves and flowers* 華 *expanding* 于 * *into full bloom.* It became a symbol for **China.** Usually, however, it is accompanied by another character 中 **Center** (originally 中 : *a target* 口 *that is pierced in the center by an arrow* |), because for the Chinese, China was the center of the World. **(Photos O, P, T)**
Often, therefore, we also find the combination 中 國 , which means **Center Country**, to stand for **China**. Originally **Country** was written 或 : *a bordered piece of land*

---

* Breath ⟩ after passing an obstacle ⟨⟩, *expanding* freely.
** See pp. **W** 4, **W** 5, **W** 12

☐ *defended by weapons (⚷ halberd) with a capital ○* (Photos D, T).

Now that we know how the Chinese write "China", we would like to know how they write **AMERICA** ! We see it on the sign for the Bank of America: 美國銀行 (**Photo D**). The last two characters mean **Bank**, we know from the above.** The second character we just met: **Country**. The first 美 means **Beautiful**. Originally written 羌 , it is composed of *sheep* 羊 (picture of a sheep, seen from behind, showing the *horns* 丷 , *four feet and tail* 干) and *big* 大 (a man with outstretched arms, as if he wants to show how big something is), to give the meaning **Beautiful**(*a big sheep being a beautiful animal*). Combining the two characters together we get **Beautiful Country**.

During our walk, we will see a number of very common characters. These are *good luck signs* that we see in the shop windows, especially those of jewelry stores. One that we very often see is 壽 **LONGEVITY** . The ancestral form is 𩵋 which consists of five symbols compressed into one. Two symbols are combined to form **Old**: *hair* 毛 and *change* 𠤎 (a man* 人 who is upside down 𠤎 , who *changed* his position), giving the idea of '*white hair*'. The third symbol 彡 represents **wrinkles** found on an old person's face. The remaining two symbols 口 *mouth* and 𠬝 *hand* are to give the idea of "making a wish using gestures", or "**to wish deeply**". To conclude therefore, we may say that the character means "**longevity following a deep wish**". (Photos V3, V5, V9)

Another character that we'll meet quite often is 囍. It means **DOUBLE JOY** and is usually used to celebrate a wedding. Invitation cards for the wedding are printed with this character, many times in gold. It is the character for **JOY** 喜 repeated twice, or 喜 in its original form, which indicates that there is *singing* (口

mouth) and *music* (a *hand* ⇗ with a *stick* — beating a *drum on a stand* 묘).(**Photos V4, V8** , where it appears on a kimono and on a porcelain pot.)

The good luck sign that can appear on almost any article is 福 for **HAPPINESS**. (**Photos V1, V7** , where it appears on a kimono, and where a porcelain statue represents a happy father blessed with a son.) We can explain its meaning by looking at the original form 禑 . The left-hand part represents a *heavenly sign* (= *heaven* , and ⫼ *what comes down from heaven*) *that brings prosperity*; the right-hand part shows *products* ○ *from the field* ⊕ *being under one's roof* ∧ .

As can be expected, the character 愛 for **LOVE** is very popular and very common. (See **Photo V2**, where it appears on a child's dress .) Looking at its ancestral form 愛 we can see the symbol for **Heart** ⿺ that we met before (in **Photo E**): it is a picture of the heart, showing the *sac* (opened), the *lobes* and the *aorta*.. Combined with 旡 **To swallow** (a *man* ⿺* *breathing in air* =), it means: **to swallow affectionate feelings down in one's heart.** The other symbol 夊 (*a man* 刀* *who advances in spite of obstacles* ⌒) is added to indicate that it is a **lingering feeling.**

Two animals that the Chinese like to use to name their businesses are the **HORSE** 馬 and the **DRAGON** 龍. The original script for the Horse is 馬 , which is a clever picture of the animal, with its mane blowing in the wind. The original form for the Dragon is 龍 . It shows on the left-hand side *the animal* 象 *flying towards the sky* = , and on the right-hand side its *wings* 戈 . The Chinese namely believed that dragons could fly towards the sky and thereby produce rain. As a rule, we find "golden" added as an adjective so that during our walk we'll find "Golden Dragon" as the name for a restaurant (**H**). The character

---

* See page W6 (Footnote).

for **GOLD** is 金, or 全 in its original form. It shows *four gold nuggets* 爰 *buried* (∧*cover*) *in the ground* *. For Horse, the adjective **PRECIOUS** 寶 is also used. The ancestral form shows *three precious possessions found in one's house* 寶 : *jade* 玉 , *porcelain* (缶 *earthenware) and money* (貝 *shell*, formerly used as money *).* (**Photos B, H, I, L**) (**Photo I, S**)

Let us now take a look at a series of characters that are commonly used by the Chinese, because they deal with the good things in life.

The character for **JOY** is 喜. We met this before in **DOUBLE JOY** (**Photos V4, V8**). Written 喜 it means: *there is music* (*a hand* ∋ *with a stick* — *beating a drum on a stand* 壴) *and singing* (口 *mouth*). (**Photo I**) Repeated twice, it is used during wedding celebrations because it is indeed a joyful event for both wife and husband.

Two other common characters 富 **WEALTHY** and 貴 **PRECIOUS, HONORABLE** appear next to each other on a sign for a flower shop. The first was originally written 富 and means: *having products* ○ *of the field* ⊕ *stacked up* ∧ *under one's roof* ∩ . The second was 貴 and means: *a basket* 坴 *containing money* (貝 *shell*, formerly used as money), or in other words 'something precious'. (**Photo R**)

---

* If used as a component in a character, it means **Metal** (*four pieces of metal ore buried in the ground*). See, e.g. **Silver**, previously discussed under **BANK**. (See page **W6**)

The next character 香 means **FRAGRANT** and is closely linked with 港 **HARBOR**, because the two combined mean **HONG KONG**. The original writing for **FRAGRANT** was 香 , meaning *the sweet* 甘 (*the mouth* 口 *holding something - agreeable) odor of grain* 禾(*a plant* 禾 *with ripening ears at the top*) *that is fermenting (vapors).* The old writing for **HARBOR** was 港 , meaning: *water* and what is commonly *used (廿 = ++ = twenty, pair of hands) in the city* (*a city* ○ *and its seal*). **(Photo M)**

And finally, one character with a very positive tone: **PEACE** 平, which was originally written , meaning *the breath going through an obstacle — and spreading out freely and evenly* . **(Photo K)**

Many times, two or more characters combine to form one meaning(as we have seen earlier with **RESTAU-RANT**, **BANK**, **FIRM**). Here are more examples that we'll meet:

SEAFOOD 海鮮 which is Sea (see p. **W 14**) and Fresh [namely, (**Fish** , picture of a Fish) and (**Sheep****), which were eaten raw by the ancient Chinese, and therefore had to be fresh].

WORLD 世界, which is **Generation** 世 (*three times ten* +, which was apparently man's life expectancy at that time) and **Boundary*** (*land (* ⊕ *field) and separation* 八 *of men*). **(Photos E, Q)**

ASIA 亞 洲 , which is 亞 (pronounced **Ya**, it is used for its pronunciation only), and **Continent** (*water* *and tracts of land through which rivers flow*). **(Photo N)**

---

* It is *man* (W6, Footnote) in a bent position .

** Picture of a sheep (seen from behind), with its *horns* , *four feet and tail* .

NEWSPAPER日報, which is **Sun, Day** ⊙ (picture of the *sun*) and **Announcement, Newspaper** 報 : *a criminal* (年 * *to offend, commit crime against man* 人) *and a hand* 乂 *holding a seal* 卩 : *an official announcement (of a judgement).*(**Photo Q**)

TRADE   CENTER   商 塲 In its original form **Trade** 商 looks like a picture of a human face. But actually it consists of three portions: 丙 *words* (*the tongue* 舌 *shown outside the mouth, and* = *the sound produced by it* ; *within* (*an object* 入 *entering a certain space* ⌒); *and two suns* ⊙⊙ (*picture of two suns*). The three portions put together mean *when words are spoken inside a room, lasting several days* : **Trade**. The second character actually means **Arena**, or **Open space.** It was formerly written 塲 and means: *land* (土 **earth)** *and* 昜 (*the sun* ㊀ *rising* ∧ *above the horizon — and its rays* 勿 *shining over an open space*). (**Photo M**)

ASSOCIATION   會 館 . The first character means **Society**, earlier written as 㑹 :*meeting* (⌒ *three lines coming together*) *and words (that* ∪ *which comes out from the mouth* ⊔) *are spoken at the fireside* (▣ *smoke outlet*) . The second character means **Restaurant**, or **Hall**, formerly written 館 : *a large building* 阝 (*building* ⌒ *with many steps* 阝)*, where food* 食 (*a pot with contents* ㊀ *, a ladle* ⼋ *, and the symbol* ∧ *to suggest 'mixing'* (three lines coming together) *is served* . (**Photo O**)

* The symbol 年 represents a *pestle*, capable of producing a grinding, unpleasant action.
** The layer = from which all things ∣ come out.

Four characters are very common, i.e. 北 **NORTH**, 南 **SOUTH**, 東 **EAST**, and 西 **WEST**. We can easily derive their meanings from their ancestral forms. **NORTH** 𣥠 : *two men turning their backs towards the North.* (Facing the South was a Chinese custom during ceremonies.) **SOUTH** 宎 : *the area* ⟩ ⟨ *where vegetation (* ψ *plant) expands continuously (* 半 *a pestle; the additional stroke* — *suggests the idea of repetition or continuity*). **EAST** 東 : *the sun* ⊕ *is in the East when it is so low that we can see it shining behind the trees* 木 *(of the Eastern mountains).* **WEST** 㢴 : *when birds* ⇶ *sit on their nests* ⊠ *it is evening and the sun is in the West.*(**Photo T** : South, North)

During our walk we'll pass the sign "Four Seas". So let us now disscuss characters which mean numbers. The Chinese have very simple symbols for the numbers **ONE**, **TWO**, and **THREE** , which are represented by *one stroke* — (一), *two strokes* 二 (二), and *three strokes* 三 (三). The numbers Four, Six and Eight are given symbols which convey the idea that they are 'even' numbers. **FOUR** 𰀁 *means a quantity that can be divided into two equal portions* (now written 四). (**Photo F**) **SIX** 𠂇 is the same symbol, but *with a dot added to distinguish it from Four.* The modern brush-written form is 六. **EIGHT** was the simple symbol)((now written 八), meaning *a quantity consisting of two equal halves.* **TEN** was a *cross* ┼ (now written 十), an appropriate symbol, because Ten is a unit. **FIVE** is also a unit in China (e.g., as used in the abacus), since we have five fingers on each hand. The old symbol was a *diagonal cross* ✕ , now 五.**SEVEN** is a unit used in fortune-telling and was written ┼ :*a cross with a "tail" to distinguish it from the unit Ten.* It is now written 七. (**Photo I**) And finally, **NINE** 九, almost the unit Ten, formerly written 𠃌 : a "wavy" ┼ (Ten).

To end our discussion, let us now take a look at a few more common characters. **RULER**, or **EMPRESS** 后 *
(*see* **Photo G**) formerly written 后 represents a *man bending over* 戶 *to give orders* (口 *mouth) to the people.*
FLOWER 花 (*see* **Photo R**) formerly written 艸 means: *that portion of plants* 丱 *that has greatly changed* 𠤎 (*a man* 人 *and* 匕 *a man-upside-down: a man who 'changed' his position).* **HERBS**, or **MEDICINE** 藥 (*see* **Photo T**), formerly written 藥 consists of two parts. The first part, the one on top, is the symbol for **grass**** 丱.
The second part 樂 looks very complicated, but it is simply a picture of a musical instrument (*a frame with a drum in the middle and bells on the sides*) and represents **Music**, or **Joy**. The two parts put together mean: *herbs (grass) that restore harmony (music, joy) in our body.* **SEA** 海 (*see* **Photo F**) was formerly written 海 . This symbol consists of three parts. One part is **Water** 水 put on the left-hand side. The second part is **Mother** 母 (*picture of a woman with prominent breasts*). The third part is **Grass** 屮, to give the idea of abundance. The three parts put together mean: *the source of all waters.* **PASTRY**, **CAKES** 餅 (*see* **Photo K**), formerly written 餅 has on the left-hand side the symbol for **Food** 食 that we have encountered many times (see pp. **W**4, **W**5, **W**12) . It represents *a pot with contents* 曰 , *a ladle* 匕 , *and the symbol* 亼 *to suggest 'mixing'* (*three lines coming together).* The right-hand part 并 means **Harmony**: *two men* 从 *marching in step* ≡ . **TO LEARN** 學 (*see* **Photo P**) , formerly written 學 represents *a child* 子 *in darkness* 冖 (*a small room)* *and two hands* 𦥑 *of the master pouring down knowledge* 爻 .

** As a rule, symbols dealing with vegetative material have the symbol for *grass* 丱 added on top.

* See page W6 (Footnote).

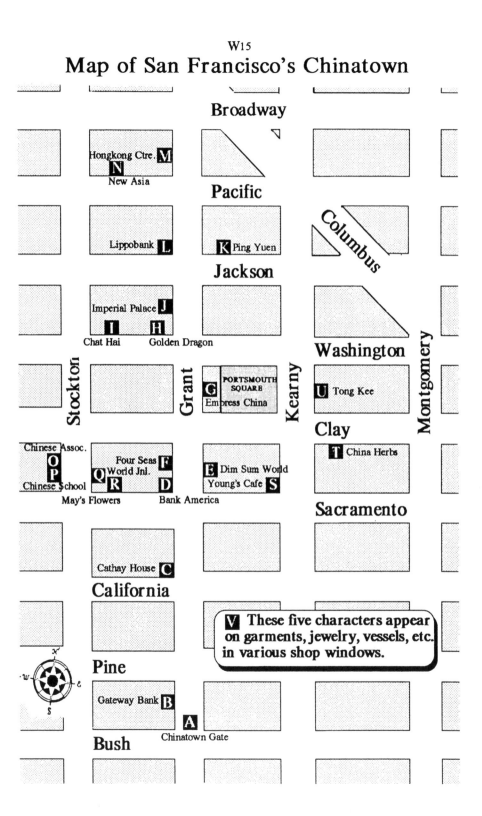

PHOTO SECTION

Let us now see the photos that were taken for the chapter *A Walk through San Francisco's Chinatown* .*
The best way is to do the Questionnaires first. Just fill in the meanings of the characters. (Numbers accompanying them refer you to the Dictionary Section.)
After this you will have no difficulties to answer the questions appearing in the text.

It would not be a bad idea at all, if you could also take the same pictures yourself! Not only you will have them in beautiful colors, but you will look at them often and help you become very familiar with the characters.

---

* For those who are in the position to do the actual walk themselves, and have a car at their disposal, there is City Public Garage ($.75 per hour) on Bush half a block away from the Chinatown Entrance Gate (Photo A).

Write in the meanings of the characters, after reading "_A Walk through San Francisco's Chinatown_ ".Or, you can also go to the _Dictionary,_ especially if you want to complete the entire Questionnaire. (Numbers accompanying the characters help you to find them in the Dictionary.)

Questionnaire on Photo A

Char- acter	Anc. Form	Meaning	Explanation
天 [8]			
下 [3]			
爲 [30]	𦥙	For (For the benefit of)	Picture of a Female Monkey, showing its Body ⌒ Claws 爫 and Breasts .
公 [5]			

A

A   Grant & Bush

This *Entrance Gate to Chinatown* bears a well-known saying by the Chinese philosopher Confucius. Freely translated it means "Under Heaven We All Must Work for the Common Good".[Find out the literal meaning of the sign on p. W3.]

The writing should be read from right to left, following the old tradition. [Read the explanation at the Footnote on p. W3]

Three of the four characters are common characters. The one that is not common is 爲 . The ancient writing represents a Female Monkey. [See the explanation on p. W3]. The original meaning is lost, but presently it could mean FOR (For the benefit of).

The character 公 is a very common character, because in combination with 司 it means FIRM or COMPANY. As can be expected, they can be seen quite often and can be spotted very easily, because they always come at the end of the sign . [Find out on pp. W5-W6 why the two put together mean Firm or Company].

The two other characters can be easily understood, once we know their original writings. [See the Dictionary for the explanations. (See the Reference Numbers accompanying the characters in the Questionnaire).]

Questionnaire on Photo B

Char-acter	Anc. Form	Meaning	Explanation
金 [20]			
門 [17]			
銀 [52]			
行 [16]			

The two characters combined 銀行 mean ....(W6)

Questionnaire on Photo C

Char-acter	Anc. Form	Meaning	Explanation
華 [39]			
園 [47]			
酒 [32]			
家 [24]			

The two characters combined 酒家 mean ....(namely, one that...(W4).

Walking up Grant Avenue, we find about halfway up the block a small bank " *Gateway Bank* " that has a beautiful sign. Here we can see how **BANK** is written in Chinese with two characters. **[Read the explanation on p. W6. Also, find out that "Gateway Bank" is not the literal translation. What should it be ? (See Questionnaire B).]**

B

541 Grant

Arriving at California street at the end of the block, we see "*Cathay House Restaurant* ", which has a beautiful tower. We will have a better and a more colorful view if we cross California street and turn around to see the restaurant tower accompanied by its twin tower on the other side of the street.

The sign tells us that in Chinese,**RESTAURANT**is written with two characters. It also tells us that this restaurant serves liquor. [**See p. W4 to know why.**]

"Cathay" is the old name for **CHINA** [**Which character is that ? See p.W7.**]

We also see a character which means **GARDEN** ; and it is used here instead of "House". [**Which one is is it? See p.W4.**]

C   718 California

Questionnaire on Photo D

Char-acter	Anc. Form	Meaning	Explanation
美²⁷			
國³⁸			

The two characters combined 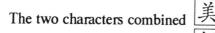 mean ....(W8)

The two characters combined 銀行 mean........................(W6)

Questionnaire on Photo E

Char-acter	Anc. Form	Meaning	Explanation
點⁶³			
心⁶			
世¹⁰			
界²⁸			

The two characters combined 點心 mean freely translated.........
...., or simply ....In Cantonese they
are pronounced "..............................." (W7).

The two characters combined 世界 mean....................(W11).

Continuing our walk along Grant, we find at the corner of Sacramento the _Bank of America,_ which has a Chinese-style column with four Chinese characters. Two of them we met earlier; together they mean **BANK** [**Which two are they? See p. W6 and Photo B.**] As can be expected the two others mean **AMERICA** [**Can you explain why ? See p. W8 .**]

A few steps further, across the street, is _"World of Pastry"_. The sign does not tell the public that the restaurant serves the popular Cantonese pastry lunch, called _Dim Sum_ , but the Chinese sign does! [**See Questionnaire E.**]

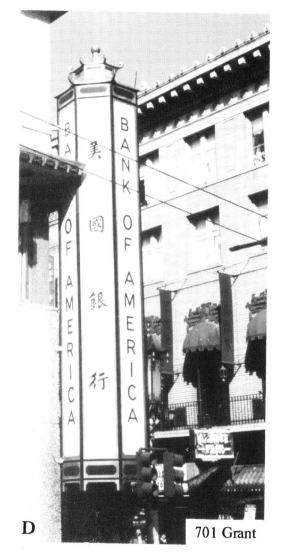

D 701 Grant

E 712 Grant

Questionnaire on Photo F

Char-acter	Anc. Form	Meaning	Explanation
四 11			
海 31			
酒 32			
樓 53			

The two characters combined: 酒樓 mean.................................
(namely, one that ....(W4).

Questionnaire on Photo G

Char-acter	Anc. Form	Meaning	Explanation
皇 29			
后 15			

The two characters combined 皇后 mean Empress (D15, D29)

The two characters combined 酒樓 mean...................(namely, one
that ....(W4.; Quest. F).

In the same block, on the left hand side, we find *"Four Seas Resaurant"*, which is a multi-story building. [This fact is indicated by which character? And does this place serve liquor? And if so, why? (W4).]

The *"Empress of China"* (next block, on right-hand side) has been visited by famous film stars and other well-known personalities,including presidents. With its exotic roof-garden, it is the highest place in Chinatown where one can have one's lunch or dinner with a sweeping view. [Same question as in previous picture: which character tells us that this restaurant is a high building with many floors , and also which character tells us that liquor is served here. (W4 & Photos F, C, H, J).]

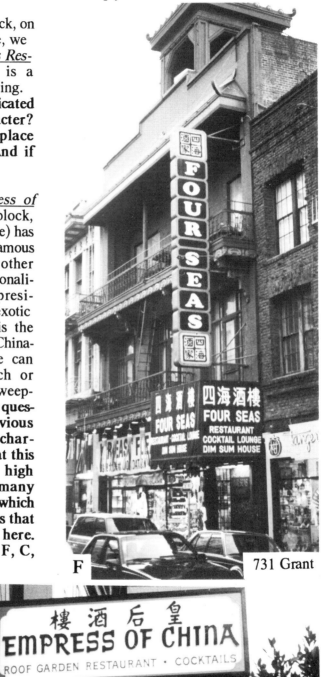

F 731 Grant

G 838 Grant

Questionnaire on Photo H

Char-acter	Anc. Form	Meaning	Explanation
金 [20]			
龍 [58]			
大 [4]			

The two characters combined 酒家 mean......................(namely, one that.......................................)(**W4**).

Questionnaire on Photo I

Char-acter	Anc. Form	Meaning	Explanation
七 [1]			
喜 [44]			
珠 [33]		*	
寶 [65]			
金 [20]			
飾 [56]			

* If standing alone, it means PEARL; if combined with 寶 [65] (VALUABLE), it means **PEARLS & JEWELS**

The two characters combined 司公 mean......................(**W 5-6**)

We now walk further to the corner of the block, where we turn left into Washington. On the right-hand side, we see the sign of a large restaurant: "*Golden Dragon Restaurant*". **[Which character means LARGE (Dict.4), and which one means DRAGON ? (W9).** We met **GOLD** at "Gateway Bank" (Photo B) but you may want to read again W10.You know the meaning of the last two characters, of course. (Photo C and W4.)

A few steps further, on the same side of the street is the "*Chat Hai Jade Jewelry Co* ." It has a sign with 8 characters. <u>Here again, we must read from right to left.</u> **(See Footnote on W3.)** The two last characters can be seen many times at the end of a sign. **[What do they mean ? (W 5-6)]**
One character that we now meet for the third time is **GOLD. (Which one is it ? If you don't know, see W10 and Photos B and H.)** The remaining five characters can be found in the Dictionary. **(See Questionnaire I for the Dictionary numbers that accompany the characters.)** You will find the explanations of their ancestral forms quite interesting. In English, the sign should actually read;"*Seven Joy Pearls, Jewels and Jewelry Company.*" **(See Footnote Questionnaire I.)**

H   816 Washington

I   864 Washington

Questionnaire on Photo J

Char-acter	Anc. Form	Meaning	Explanation
皇 [29]			
宮 [34]			

The two characters combined 酒家 mean........................(namely, one that...(**W4**).

Questionnaire on Photo K

Char-acter	Anc. Form	Meaning	Explanation
平 [14]			
園 [47]			
餅 [57]			
家 [24]			

650 Jackson

K   PING YUEN

J   919 Grant *Cocktails*

Coming back to Grant, we walk upwards toward Jackson. On the left-hand side is "*Imperial Palace*". We notice that the sign here is written in ancient script. We recognize that the last two characters mean **RESTAURANT**. So, the first two characters must mean **IMPERIAL PALACE**. [**Find out why.** (Photo G, Dict. 29) (Dict. 34)]

Arriving at the crossing with Jackson and without going into it, we see on the left-hand side the sign for "*Ping Yuen Restaurant* ". We have met the fourth character already, because it is part of the pair which means **RESTAURANT**. [**What does it mean?** (W4, Dict. 24)] We have also met before the second character [**What does it mean?** (Photo C, W4).]

The first character means **PEACE** and the third character means **PASTRY** [**Find out why.** (Dict. 14) (Dict. 57)

Incidentally, the English translation of the sign would be "*Peace Garden Pastry House*".

Questionnaire on Photo L

Character	Anc. Form	Meaning	Explanation
金 20			
山 2			

The two characters combined 銀行 mean.....................(W6).

The two characters combined 金山 mean: SAN FRANCISCO
("Gold Mountain" for the Chinese).

Questionnaire on Photo M

Character	Anc. Form	Meaning	Explanation
香 25			
港 42			
商 37			
塲 54			

The two characters combined 香港 mean ....(W11)

The two characters combined 商塲 mean.......................(W12)

Staying at the corner of Grant and Jackson, we see on our left-hand side the sign " *Lippobank* ". The first character we now see for the fourth time ! [**What does it mean ?** (Photos B, H, I and W10) .] The second character is also a very common character. It means **MOUNTAIN** [**Find out the explanation why.** (Dict. 2).] and it is important, because combined with GOLD, the two mean: GOLD MOUNTAIN, which is the Chinese name for **SAN FRANCISCO**!

L   1001 Grant   M   1136 Grant

The two last characters combined we see all the time also. [Because they mean ? (Photos B, D & W6).]

The next sign we see is on the next block, again on the left-hand side of the street.* The first two characters are important; in combination they mean **HONG KONG**. [Find out what "Hong Kong" means in Chinese (or rather Cantonese, to be exact). (W11).] The last two characters combined mean TRADE CENTER [Explain why this is so. (W12).]

* Grant Avenue being a one-way street, with most traffic going by on the right-hand side of the street, the important stores are apparently situated on the left-hand side, because while driving by, the ones on the right side are difficult to see.

Questionnaire on Photo N

Char-acter	Anc. Form	Meaning	Explanation
新 [49]			
亞		A "phonetic"	Used for its pronunciation "Ya".
洲 [23]			

The two characters combined 亞洲 mean................... (**W11**)

Questionnaire on Photo O

Char-acter	Anc. Form	Meaning	Explanation
中 [9]			
華 [39]			
會 [48]			
館 [61]			

The two characters combined 中華 mean ....(**W7**)

The two characters combined 會館 mean ....(**W12**)

We now go into Pacific. Immediately, our attention is drawn to the *"New Asia" Restaurant* *, which is festively decorated with nu-erous flags on its roof.

* *"New Asia"* is one of the places in Chinatown, where a complete *Dim Sum* lunch is served. *Dim Sum* is served only during lunch and consists of various snacks, such as pork buns, shrimp and meat dumplings, egg rolls, turnovers.
In the larger places, the various food assortments are wheeled around on tea
. Waitresses call out the names of the items to bring them to the attention

On its lantern we see three important characters.[**Which one means <u>NEW</u> ? (Dict. 49).**] The second and third characters form a pair, and mean <u>ASIA</u>. The <u>second character</u> is only used for its pronunciation: *"Ya"* (short for *"A-si-ya"*), while the <u>third character</u> means **Continent [see explanations at W11 and at Dict. 23.]**

Continuing our walk along Pacific, we reach Stockton. Here we turn left and walk four blocks until we are facing the beautiful building of the *"<u>Chinese Association</u>"*. The sign contains four characters painted in gold. Again, we have to *read the old-fashioned way: from right to left* (**Footnote on W3**).

There are two pairs of characters here: one pair means <u>**CHINA**</u> [**Which ones? (W7).**]; the other pair means <u>**ASSOCIATION**</u> (**see W12**).

772 Pacific

N

O

843 Stockton

Questionnaire on Photo P

Char-acter	Anc. Form	Meaning	Explanation
中 [9]			
華 [39]			
學 [60]			
校 [36]			

The two characters combined 中華 mean ....(W7)

The two characters combined 學校 mean SCHOOL ("Learning School", literally).

Questionnaire on Photo Q

Char-acter	Anc. Form	Meaning	Explanation
世 [10]			
界 [28]			
日 [7]			
報 [41]			

The two characters combined 世界 mean ....(W11)

The two characters combined 日報 mean ....(W12)

Next to the *"Chinese Society"* is the *"Chinese School "* - also a beautiful building in Chinese style. *Reading the sign from right to left* (**see Footnote on W3**), we can distinguish two pairs of characters. The first pair is the same as the first pair on the sign of the *"Chinese Society "*. It means namely **CHINA** (W7). The second pair means **SCHOOL**, of which the first character means **LEARN** (W14) and the second means **SCHOOL** (**Dict. 36**).

P   829 Stockton

Before leaving Stockton, we take a look at *"World Journal"* across the street. Again, *reading from right to left* (**Footnote W3**) we distinguish two pairs of characters, of which the first means **WORLD** and the second means **NEWS** (**you find the explanations on** W11 **and** W12).

Q   824 Stockton

Questionnaire on Photo R

Char-acter	Anc. Form	Meaning	Explanation
富 45			
貴 43			
花 19			
店 21			

Questionnaire on Photo S

Char-acter	Anc. Form	Meaning	Explanation
寶 65			
馬 22			
海 31			
鮮 62			
餐 59			
廳 68			

The two characters combined 海鮮 mean.....................(W 11)

The two characters combined 餐廳 mean.....................(W 5).

Going down Stockton a few steps, brings us to the crossing of Stockton and Sacramento. We now turn left into Sacramento, heading toward Kearny. Halfway down the block, we see "*May's Flower Shop*" on our left-hand side. [**Explain why the Chinese sign is quite different than the English sign ! (What do the first two characters mean ? < See Questionnaire R for references to the Dictionary. >)**

R   872 Sacramento

After crossing Grant, we arrive at the corner of Sacramento and Kearny. At this corner, we find " *Young's Cafe* ". It's sign has six characters. No.3 and No.4 form a pair, which in English means SEA-FOOD (W11).

Nos. 5 and 6 are also a pair: it means simply RESTAURANT. But one that is "dignified" (W5).

The English sign is quite different than the Chinese sign. [**What does the Chinese sign mean ? [(What do No. 1 and No.2 mean ? < See Questionnaire S >) (What do No.3 and No.4 combined mean? (See above.)]**

S   601 Kearny

Questionnaire on Photo T

Char-acter	Anc. Form	Meaning	Explanation
中 [9]			
國 [38]			
南 [26]			
北 [13]			
藥 [64]			
材 [18]			
行 [16]			

The two characters combined 中國 mean........................(**W** 7-8)

Questionnaire on Photo U

Char-acter	Anc. Form	Meaning	Explanation
粥 [40]			
麵 [66]			
飯 [46]			

From the corner, we walk toward Portsmouth Square and stop at another corner:Kearny & Clay. Looking down Clay we can see *"China Herbs"* with its long vertical sign.We see seven characters.

The first two mean **CHINA** (Explain: why? (W 7-8).) No. 3 and No. 4 mean **SOUTH** and **NORTH** [**Find out the reasons why (W**13 **).**] Then follow No. 5, which means **HERBS** or **MEDICINE** (W14) and No.6, which means **MATERIAL** (Dict. 18). And lastly, No.7, which we met before. [**What does it mean? (See Photos B, D and L.)**]

Walking a little bit further, we see across the street (a bit hidden behind a glass bus-shelter) three large characters written at the bottom of a restaurant. They are important, very common characters in a restaurant. [**What do they mean? What do they want to tell the passersby ? (See W**6-7**.)**]

T Clay & Kearny

U 710 Kearny

Window-shopping along Grant, we see many stores showing garments, jewelry, statues and other items in their windows. Interesting for us are the ones that have *Good Luck Signs* on them. **[Which *Good Luck Signs* do you see in Photos V1, V2, V3 and V4 ? Give also explanations based on their ancestral forms (See W8, W9, W10).]**

Questionnaire on Photo V1

Char- acter	Anc. Form	Meaning & Explanation
福 [50]		

Questionnaire on Photo V2

Char- acter	Anc. Form	Meaning & Explanation
愛 [51]		

Questionnaire on Photo V3

Char- acter	Anc. Form	Meaning & Explanation
壽 [55]		

Questionnaire on Photo V4

Char- acter	Anc. Form	Meaning & Explanation
囍 [67]		

V1

V2

V3

V4

These three statues seen here are to bring **Good Luck** to the Family
[Complete *all* boxes in Questionnaire V5, V6, V7. (See the references to the Dictionary.)]

Questionnaire on Photos *V5, V6, V7*

Pho-to	Char-acter	Anc. Form	Meaning	Explanation
	壽 55			
	財 35			
	福 50			

Complete *all* boxes in Questionnaires V8 and V9.

Questionnaire on Photo *V8*

Character	Ancestral Form	Meaning & Explanation
囍 67		

Questionnaire on Photo *V9* [What Character does the symbol represent ?

Character	Ancestral Form	Meaning & Explanation
55		

| V5 | *Longevity* | V6 | *Wealth* | V7 | *Happiness* |

V8

V9

DICTIONARY SECTION

The following 68 characters appear on the signs discussed in *A Walk through San Francisco's Chinatown.* They are arranged according to the number of strokes. (The stroke numbers appear at the left margin.)

2			
Symbol for a Unit used in Divination [with a 'tail' to distinguish it from **Ten** (+)]. *1* [Photo I] **Seven**			
3			
Picture of a Mountain. *2* [Photo L] **Mountain**			
An object | Below a certain level ⎯. *3* [Photo A] **Below. Under**			
A Man with Outstretched Arms, as if showing how large something is. *4* [Photo H] **Large. Big**			
4			
Distribution ﾉﾍ of a Private Possession (ㅎ Cocoon; with the self-enclosed silk-worm it gives the idea of privacy). *5* [Photos A, I] **Public. Common**			

Picture of the Heart, showing the Sac opened; the Lobes and Aorta are also seen. *6* [Photo E] **Heart**		
Picture of the Sun. *7* [Photo Q] **Sun. Day**		
That which expands ― over Man 人 . *8* [Photo A] **Heaven**		
A Target ☐ pierced in the Center by an Arrow │ . *9* [Photos O, P, T] **Center**		
Three times Ten ＋ : which was apparently man's life expectancy at that time. *10* [Photos E, Q] **Generation**		

5		
A quantity that can be divided into two equal portions. *11* [Photo F] ***Four***		
A Man 𝄫* bending over ⌐ to shout his orders (⊌ Mouth). *12* [Photo I] ***Manage (v).*** ***Administration***		
Two Men turning their backs towards the North)(\((Facing the South was a Chinese custom during ceremonies.) *13* [Photo T] ***North***		
The Breath ∮ going through an Obstacle — and spreading out evenly π. *14* [Photo K] ***Even. Peace***		
6		
A Person 𝄫* Bending Over ⌐ to give orders (⊔ Mouth) to the people. *15* [Photo G] ***Ruler. Empress***		

* A being that has two legs - only the legs are portrayed.

Footsteps made by the Left and Right Feet: a place where people come and go. **16** [Photos B, D, L, T] ***Store***		
7 *Picture of 'Saloon-Door' with swinging leaves.* **17** [Photo B] ***Door. Gate***		
Symbol for Wood 朩*, and* 千 *as "phonetic".* [See <u>NOTE 1</u>, at No. 33.] **18** [Photo T] ***Material******		
8 *The portion of plants* ΨΨ *that has greatly changed (* 𠤎 *To change*).* **19** [Photo R] ***Flower***		
Four Nuggets ꜀꜀ *buried (* ∧ *To cover) in the Earth* ⊥***.* ***Metal.*** **20** [Photos B, H, I, L] ***Gold***		

* *A Man* 儿 *(a being that has two legs - only the legs are portrayed) and a Man-Upside Down* 𠤎 *: a man who "changed" his position.*

** *The Layer* ⸗ *from which all Things* 丨 *come out.*

*** *Material for building (timber, etc.)*

A Dwelling ⌒ in which Divination* 卜 is practiced. **21**　[Photo R]　***Shop***		
Picture of a Horse, with mane blowing in the wind. **22**　[Photo S]　***Horse***		
Water and Three Islets ⦰⦰⦰ around which Water 川 flows.** **23**　[Photo N]　***Continent***		
A Dwelling ⌒ where Pigs 豕 have free entry***. 　　　　　　***House(hold).*** **24** [Photos C, H, J, K]　***Home***		
The Sweet (the Mouth ⊔ holding something agreeable −) Odor of Fermented (⌃ Vapors) Grain 禾 . **25**　[Photo M]　***Fragrant***		

* The symbol ⊢ represents 'cracks' caused by heating tortoise shells. Divination (fortune-telling) was spoken out (⊔ Mouth) after closely studying the cracks.
** The symbol 川 (many islets combined) could also be interpreted as a large island (continent).
*** To make sure that they were adequately fed, pigs had the same privileges as dogs today.

The area)(where vegetation (ψ Plant) expands continuously (干 Pestle; the additional stroke – suggests continuity). **26** [Photo T] ***South***		南
*As is a Big Sheep (大 Big[4]; Sheep 羊 *) with fully developed horns.* **27** [Photo D] ***Beautiful***		美
Land (⊕ Field) and Separation 八 of Men ⺈ (儿 Man,+ compressed). **28** [Photos E, Q] ***Boundary***		界
*King (王[65], the precious stone that only Kings could possess) from the very beginning (自 Nose**).* **29** [Photos G, J] ***Imperial***		皇
Picture of a Female Monkey, showing its Claws 爪, Body 人 and Breasts ƍƍ. **30** [Photo A] ***For******		爲

* Picture of a Sheep (seen from behind: the Horns ᵛ, Four Feet and Tail 干).

** According to the Chinese, the Nose was the first part of the body to develop in human embryo.

*** ***For the benefit of***, which is one of the present meanings of this character. *The original meaning seems to be lost.*

\+ A being that has two legs - only the legs are portrayed.

10			
The symbol for Water 𝄂 and 𝄂 Every **. *31* [Photos F, S] **Sea**			
A Wine Jar and its contents (Water, Liquor). **Liquor.** *32* [Photos C, F, G, H, J] **Wine**			
A precious stone (王 *Jade) and 朱 as the "phonetic" (NOTE 1 below). *33* [Photo I] **Pearl**			
A Dwelling ∩ containing a Series of Rooms 吕 . *34* [Photo J] **Palace**			
A Hand acquiring Money (Shell, which formerly was used for money). *35* [Photo V9] **Wealth**			

* See Footnote at No. 65.
** The *bottom part* of this symbol is Mother, because the sea is the 'mother' of all waters. The *top part* is ψ Grass, to suggest that it is found in abundance.

NOTE 1: Not all characters are 'pictograms', and can be explained through pictures. Many characters consist of two symbols: one gives the "idea" and the other serves as a "phonetic" (gives the pronunciation).

+ A Woman with prominent breasts.

A Building (米 Tree, because it is made of wood) and 仌 as "phonetic" part (NOTE 1, at No. 33). *36*　　[Photo P]　　***School***		
Where Words * 舌 are spoken (口 Mouth) Within 内 ** a room, lasting several days (⊙ Sun). *37*　　[Photo M]　　***Trade***		
Country ☐ with its Capital o that is defended by Weapons (戈 Halberd). *38*　　[Photos D, T]　**Country**		
Glorious Country : Leaves and Flowers 华 that are Expanding 亏 (Breath ✓ after passing an Obstacle ═, expanding freely) into full bloom. *39*　[Photos C, O, P]　**China**		
Rice*** 米 that is thoroughly Boiled (弜 Steam coming from the boiling water). *40*　　[Photo U]　　***Porridge***		

* The Tongue 舌 and the Sound ═ being produced by it.
** An Object Entering 入 a certain Space ∩.
*** Four Grains of Rice, that is Scattered 乂 due to Thrashing 十.

A Criminal (ⵤ* Offend, commit crime against Man 大) and a Hand 彐 holding a Seal 卪 : an Official Announcement (of a judgement). **Announcement.** *41* [Photo N] **Newspaper**		
Water 氵 and 㬅 What is Commonly Used (廿 = 十 十 = Twenty ; 𦥑 Pair of Hands) in the City 邑 (City 口 and its Seal 卪). ┐ *42* [Photo M] **Harbor**		
A Basket 𠀉 containing Money (貝 Shell, which was formerly used as money). **Honorable.** *43* [Photo R] **Costly. Precious**		
There is Singing (口 Mouth) and Music (a Hand 彐 holding a Stick – beating a Drum-on-a-Stand 豆). *44* [Photo I] **Joy**		
Having Products 口 of the Field ⊕ Stacked Up 入 under one's Roof 宀. *45* [Photo R] **Wealthy**		

* The symbol ⵤ represents a Pestle (capable of producing a grinding, offensive action.

13

Symbol for Food ⟨glyph⟩ * *and a Hand* ⟨glyph⟩ *in Motion* ⟨glyph⟩, *bringing the food into the mouth.* **Food.** *46* [Photo U] **Rice (cooked)**	⟨glyph⟩	⟨glyph⟩
A Fence □ *and a Long Robe* ⟨glyph⟩ **, *because the long vines in the garden give the impression that the trees put on robes.* *47* [Photos C, K] **Garden**	⟨glyph⟩	⟨glyph⟩
A Meeting (⟨glyph⟩ *three lines coming together) where Words (* ⟨glyph⟩ *that which comes out from the Mouth* ⟨glyph⟩ *) are spoken at the Fireside (*⟨glyph⟩ *Smoke Outlet).* *48* [Photo O] **Society**	⟨glyph⟩	⟨glyph⟩
New branches Cut (⟨glyph⟩ *Axe) from the Hazel Tree (* ⟨glyph⟩ *Tree;* ⟨glyph⟩ *Offend***). (Only 'newly' cut branches of this tree were used to beat criminals).* *49* [Photo N] **New**	⟨glyph⟩	⟨glyph⟩
Heavenly sign ⟨glyph⟩ *(= Heaven;* ⟨glyph⟩ *Emanations from Heaven) that brings Prosperity (Products* ○ *of the Field* ⊕ *under one's Roof* ⟨glyph⟩ *).* **Happiness.** *50* [Photo V1] **Good Fortune**	⟨glyph⟩	⟨glyph⟩

* A Pot with Contents ⟨glyph⟩, a Ladle ⟨glyph⟩, and Mixing ⟨glyph⟩ (three lines coming together).
** Robe (cloth hanging over one's shoulder ⟨glyph⟩) so long that it 'drags' [an Ox (represented by its Horn ⟨glyph⟩) equipped for 'dragging' (⟨glyph⟩ Hook) the plow] over the floor.
*** The symbol ⟨glyph⟩ represents a Pestle, capable of producing a grinding, unpleasant action) ; one's Superior ⟨glyph⟩.

14

To Swallow ⌂ * affectionate feelings down in one's Heart ⌂ [6]. (The symbol ⌂ ** is added to indicate that it is a lingering feeling.) 51　　[Photo V2]　　**Love**		
Symbol for a Metal ⌂ [20] and Defiance ⌂ ***, because Silver is malleable (defies the action of a hammer). 52　　[Photos B, D, L]　　**Silver**		
Building (⌂ Tree, Wood) and as 'phonetic" [NOTE 1, at No.33] ⌂ (a Woman ⌂ Locked Up ⌂ in a Lofty Palace Prison ⌂ for misbehavior). 　　　　　　　　　　**Multi-** 53　[Photos F, G]**Story House**		
Ground (⌂ Earth, the Layer ⌂ from which all Things ⌂ come out) and ⌂ the Sun ⌂ Rising ⌂ above the Horizon — and its Rays ⌂ shining down on the Open Space　　　　**Arena.** 54　　[Photo M]　**Open Space**		
White Hair ⌂ ****; Furrows (⌂ Wrinkles) and To Implore [To Beg (⌂ Mouth) with Gesture (⌂ Hand), i.e. Longevity following a Deep Wish. 55　　[Photo V5]　　**Longevity**		

* A Man ⌂ (⌂ the two Legs of a man) breathing in Air ⌂.
** A Man ⌂ (the two Legs of a man) who Advances, in spite of an Obstacle ⌂ .
*** A Man ⌂ (the two Legs of a Man) Turning Around ⌂ , in order to Look(⌂ Eye) another Man 'defiantly' in the eye.
****Hair ⌂ that has Changed ⌂ (a Man ⌂ Upside Down: who 'changed' his position)

To scrub the animal [a Man ʮ (⌁⁺modified) with a piece of Cloth ⋔ ***] before offering it to the Gods (⍋* Food). **56** [Photo I] **Ornament**		
The symbol for Food* ⍋ and ⾕(Two Man Marching in Harmony, suggesting that cakes are a harmonious mixture of ingredients.) **57** [Photo K] **Cakes. Pastry**		
A Dragon ⍭ flying towards the Sky = and its Wings ⍩ . (It was believed that Dragons could fly towards the sky and thereby produced rain.)** **58** [Photo H] **Dragon**		
Food ⍋* and To Consume ⍝ (a Hand ⍒ and a Skeleton ⍊ left after the flesh is consumed) **59** [Photo S] **Meal**		
The Child ⍦ in Darkness (∩ Small Room) and the Two ⊦⊰ Hands of the Master pouring Knowledge ⍺ to him. **60** [Photos P] **Learn**		

* See Footnote at No. 46.
** And when it was hidden in the well, there was draught.
*** A Duster, a piece of Cloth hanging from the girdle, ready for use.
+ A being that has two legs - only the legs are portrayed.

17 *A Large Building* 🏛 *(Building with many Steps* 🏛 *), where Food* 🍱 *(see Footnote, No. 59) is served.* **61** [Photo O] ***Cultural Center***		
Fish 🐟 *and Sheep* ⼨ **, which were eaten raw by the ancient Chinese, and therefore had to be fresh.* **62** [Photo S] ***Fresh***		
Soot ⴉ *deposited around the Vent* ⬭ *by a Smoky Fire* 🔥 *** and* ⵊ *as 'phonetic'.* [NOTE 1, at No. 33]. **63** [Photo E] ***Speck. Dot***		
19 *Herbs (* ⵝⵝ *Grass) that restore Harmony (* ⵝ *Musical Instru-ment***).* **64** [Photo T]***Herbs. Medicine***		
Precious Possessions in one's House ⌂ *: Jade* 王 *****, Por-celain (* ⊕ *Earthenware) and Money (* 貝 *Shell, which was formerly used as money).* **65** [Photos I, S] ***Precious***		

* Picture of a Sheep, seen from behind: the Horns ⵉ , Four Feet and Tail ⼨ .
** Pile of Wood burning with Flames 火 (repeated twice).
*** A Frame with a Drum (*in the middle*) and Bells (*on the sides*).
**** Three Pieces of Jade 三 on a String ｜ .

20			
Wheat 麥 * *and* 回 *as the 'phonetic'* (see Footnote, No. 59). **66** [Photo U] ***Noodles***			

| 24 | *Joy* 喜 ⁴⁴ *repeated twice.*

 67 [Photo V8] ***Double Joy*** | | |

| 25 | *Shelter* 广 *and as 'phonetic'* (see Footnote, No. 59) 聽 *Hear* (*because musical performance often takes place in a Hall*).
 68 [Photo S] ***Hall. Parlor*** | | |

* A Plant 朮 with Ears of Grain ⋏⋏; and 夂 representing a Man⁺ 刀 who advances in spite of Obstacles ⌒, indicating the relentless development of the grain.

⁺ A being that has two legs - only the legs are portrayed.

General Index*

* References to the Photos are given in the Dictionary.